GIMME YOUR LUNCH MONEY:
Heartland Poets Speak out against Bullies

GIMME YOUR LUNCH MONEY: *Heartland Poets Speak out against Bullies*

Edited by
Dennis Etzel, Jr.
and
Lindsey Martin-Bowen

PaLadiN CoNteMporaries * Scottsdale * Kansas City, Missouri

© 2016 by Paladin Contemporaries

All rights for individual poems revert to individual poets in this collection. Except for brief quotations embodied in critical articles and reviews in newspapers, magazines, radio, or television, no part of this book may be reproduced in any form or by any means, electronic, mechanical, or by any information storage and retrieval system without the written permission from the individual authors—or as a collection, from the publisher.

For information and permission, contact

Paladin Contemporaries
6117 Nisbet Road
Scottsdale, AZ 85354

Library of Congress Cataloguing-in-Publication Data
Etzel, Jr., Dennis, and Lindsey Martin-Bowen, editors.

GIMME YOUR LUNCH MONEY: Heartland Poets Speak out against Bullies and Bullying/Dennis Etzel, Jr. and Lindsey Martin-Bowen, Editors, First Edition.

ISBN-13 978-1-881048-10-7
ISBN-10 1-881048-10-1

1. Poetry. 2. Psychology. 3. Sociology.

Paladin Contemporaries: Scottsdale, Arizona. Kansas City, Missouri.

For victims of bullying and persecution worldwide, including those who suffered as victims of terrorist attacks, perpetuated by armed bullies.

Acknowledgments

Thanks to the editors and publishers of the publications where the following poems first appeared.

Roy Beckemeyer's "Lessons" and "*The Baltimore Catachism*: 'Who Made the World?'" *Music I Once Could Dance To*" (Coal City Press 2014).

Pat Daneman's "Boys Who Cut the Legs off Box Turtles," *RE: Arts and Letters* (Winter/Spring 2008).

Dennis Etzel, Jr.'s "Cleaning the Flat Grill," *seveneightfive*, and *Fast-Food Sonnets* (Coal City Press 2016). "from *The Sum of Two Mothers*," *Indiana Review*, and *The Sum of Two Mothers* (ELJ Publications 2013).

Tina Hacker's "A Jewish Girl Ponders Skin," *Shot Glass Journal*, Issue 8 (September 2012), "Dinner Out," *WordWright*, (September/October 2000).

Robert Haynes's "She Who Had Nothing to Lose," *Hiram Poetry Review* (2013). "A Man that Mad Don't Fan Himself," *Lake Effect, A Journal of the Literary Arts* (2006). "Force of the Sonogram," *Baltimore Review* (1987).

Christopher Howell's "Mean and Stupid," *A New Geography of Poets* (University of Arkansas Press 1993). The poem also has been published "several times," Howell said. Reprinted with the author's permission.

Melissa Fite Johnson's "High School Pep Band," *Red eft Review* (December 29, 2015) and *Ghost Sign* (forthcoming). "On Ray Rice," *TheNewVerse.News* (Nov. 18, 2014), "Nineteen," (*Cow Creek Review* 2003). "Halloween 2014," *The 365 Anthology* (forthcoming).

Gary Lechliter's "Incident at Rider's Ford," *Off the Beaten Path* (Woodley 2014) and *The Kansas City Voices* (November 2012).

Lindsey Martin-Bowen's "The Big C," *Inside Virgil's Garage* (Chatter House Press 2013).

Caryn Mirriam-Goldberg's "What I Could Tell," *Animals in the House* (Woodley Press 2004)

Ki Russell's "Bath," "The Antler Woman Responds," and "Infactuectomy," *The Antler Woman Responds* (Paladin Contemporaries 2014).

Alarie Tennille's "Summer 1970, the University of Virginia Opens to Women in the Fall," *Southern Women's Review* (2015).

Maryfrances Wagner's "Mending Leroy's Sweater in Composition" and "Kastavas Puts It on the Line," *Dioramas* (Mammoth Publications 2015).

Photograph, page 18, by Ki Russell.
Photograph, page 48, by Lindsey Martin-Bowen.

Whether it's the boy shaking a fist and demanding a youth's lunch money—or today, a Smart phone or Nintendo—or the boss who won't listen to employees, bullies and bullying come in wide varieties—and at all levels of society. We see political bullying at local, regional, national, global levels. And perhaps because many poets' personalities tend toward the eccentric (conformity remains far too challenging for them), they have often become victims of bullying, in a multitude of forms. Here, poets have spoken out against this pervasive evil in their poems, which range from illustrating bullying, not only childhood/adolescent bullying, but may include bullying in the workplace, in culture, in politics, in facing the -isms (sexism, racism, ageism, ableism, etc.), religion, marital status, military service status, animals, and even in scientific labs for humanity's "greater good." Bullies can be diseases (such as cancer). And voices in our heads can bully us.

Ronda Miller, one of the poets in this volume, aptly defined varieties of bullies and forms of bullying:

> some are sly
> with different hues
> and degrees like
> a sunset or the sky.
> Some come earnestly.
> A "friend" laughs,
> pokes your stomach,
> says you're fat.
> They make excuses,
> it's okay, they say,
> for me to tell you that
> because I know you well.
> Another adjusts your dress
> as if what you wear upsets,
> causes distress. I say,
> if it's not a compliment,
> keep it within
> rather than without . . .

Some of these poems evoke empathy for bullies, too, revealing a keen insight that many bullies were once victims of bullies. We selected the best and most diverse work we received from accomplished poets who were either victims of bullying because of their color, disabilities, because they are members of ethnic minorities, foreign-born residents, LGBTQ persons, or veterans—or because they witnessed those injustices and spoke out against the abuse. We thank them for their superb contributions to this collection.

Editors:

Dennis Etzel Jr,
Author, *Fast-Food Sonnets*,
The Sum of Two Mothers,
My Secret Wars of 1984.

Lindsey Martin-Bowen,
Author, *CROSSING KANSAS
with Jim Morrison*,
Inside Virgil's Garage,
Standing on the Edge of the World.

Contents

Barry R. Barnes, "Shadow," 15
    "Why," 16
    "Down Alleyways," 17

Roy Beckemeyer, "First Holy Communion," 19
    "For Billie," 20
    "Lessons," 20
    "*The Baltimore Catechism*: 'Who Made the World?'" 21

James Benger, "Rufus," 22
    "He Like Nothing," 23
    "Reach Down," 24
    "Freedom Run," 25
    "Grateful," 26

Annette Billings, "Now What?" 27

Wayne Courtois, "Coriolis," 28

Pat Daneman, "The Boys Who Cut the Legs off Box Turtles," 32

Dennis Etzel Jr., "from *Robinson Middle Sham*," 34
    "Cleaning out the Flat Grill," 35

Gu Jieming Gulley, "I Could Tell He Was Trying to Sing," 36

Tina Hacker, "A Jewish Girl Ponders Skin," 37
    "Not a Crime," 38
    "Dinner Out," 39

Robert Haynes, "She Who Had Nothing to Lose," 40
    "A Man that Mad Don't Fan Himself," 41
    "Force of the Sonogram," 42

Melissa Fite Johnson, "High School Pep Band," 43
    "On Ray Rice," 44
    "Nineteen," 45

"Halloween 2014," 46

Gary Lechliter, "Them Folks," 47
"Skidmore," 49
"Incident at Rider's Ford," 50

Denise Low, "Music Lessons," 51

Goldie Manasseh, "Circumstantial Bully," 52

Lindsey Martin-Bowen, "The Big C," 54
"Jim Morrison Rescues Me," 55

Ronda Miller, "Among the Wild Primrose," 56
"Born to Bully," 58
"Every Thing They Had," 59

Caryn Mirriam-Goldberg, "Happiness," 60
"What I Could Tell," 61

Eve Ott, "Once upon a Time," 62
"Pedal Harder," 63
"My Bully," 64

Shawn Pavey, "Paying Up," 67

Dan Pohl, "Eighteen Moves to Checkmate," 68
"Drones," 70
"For Those Who Can Relate," 72
"Fifties Tourists," 73
"Why the Drama of the Socially Puzzled," 74

Jeanette Powers. "Family Tradition," 75

Kevin Rabas, "Ring-cut," 77

Carl Rhoden, "Miguel's Story," 78
"Guns Beer Liquor Ammo Ice," 79
"Where Did the Body Come from?" 80
"She Still Cannot Speak," 81

Ki Russell, "Bath," 83
    "The Antler Woman Responds," 84
    "Infactuectomy," 85

Ralph Seligman-Courtois, "Table Tennis Tournament," 86
    "Erosion," 87
    "Clover So Fragrant," 88
    "To the Rescue," 89
    "Bully vs. Ally," 90

Tyler Sheldon, "Growing Up Free," 91

Alarie Tennille, "She Doesn't Have to Call Me a Bitch," 92
    "Summer 1970, The University of Virginia Opens to Women in the Fall," 93

Maryfrances Wagner, "Mending Leroy's Sweater in Composition," 94
    "Kastavas Puts It on the Line," 95

Diane Wahto, "The Yellow Dress," 96
    "Watching *Apocalypse Now* with My Friend Dave," 97

Laura Madeline Wiseman, "Original Trolls," 98
    "Inside the Rooted Passage," 99

Christopher Howell (a special submission by Gary Lechliter, with the author's permission), "Mean and Stupid," 100

Barry R. Barnes

SHADOW

There is a shadow
It looms over the playground
Sunshine rain it's always around
It only seems to know pain
It hides in the corner of classrooms
You can't see it but I know it's there
Judging what I wear
How I wear my hair
It looms large in the halls
Maybe today
It will not hit me in the head with a ball
Small weak slow you're a target
It says after each blow
It all hurts words fist
It even takes jabs at me over the Internet
All most any of us want
Is to fit in
We could even be friends
So you act cool keep quiet
Pray that it ends
No one should ever be forced to fight
And everyone is entitled to light

WHY

Why am I like this
Why does this happen to me
There you are
Thought you could get away
Caught you
Now you're going to have to pay
Pay for being you
Wrong place wrong time
People say don't know why I act this way
I would take other kids' toys
Candy money
Push them away
My parents would say
Boys will be boys
That's the way kids play
Ignore it Stand up for yourself
Easier said than done
Sometimes your only choice
Is to run
Hurting others shouldn't be fun
But I do what I do
Spread blues
Bullies are made some born that way
Seems impossible to stop
No matter how hard we try
The persecutor
The victim
All in pain
We must never stop looking for answers
We must keep asking why

DOWN ALLEYWAYS

Side streets
Through the woods
Hide behind trees
Don't know why those kids are so mean
Don't know why they pick on me
They got little Billy the other day
Was not fast enough to run away
Silently lick your wounds
Bruises bumps cutting words
Saw Susie Sunday afternoon
She was crying on the curb
Had been pushed around
In the basement of our church
People people be aware
Bullies can be anywhere
Bathroom cloakroom
In the halls on the stairs
On your phone in your home

Roy Beckemeyer

FIRST HOLY COMMUNION

(After a Photo of the St. Anthony's Parochial School Second Grade Class members on the day of their First Holy Communion, 1948)

The Word of God, children of God, white
as the driven snow, so bright that God's sun
makes each face appear to hover
in the dazzling air, angelic, perplexed,
worried, content, already floating as if
to set off heavenward. A day of peace.

But the truce would be broken
on the playground at lunch tomorrow
by the one kid unwilling to change,
unable to float skyward, still anchored
by the need to bully. His slight smile
already angling toward his trademark
smirk, here on the very day when God
came and sat on his tongue, and he
swallowed, waiting for the lightning
that never came, knowing now that
he could continue to be himself, as he
had always been, as he was now,
would be tomorrow,
and forevermore.

FOR BILLIE

On her hundredth birthday, April 7, 2015

Smoke, shadowed mirror, gardenia at your ear. Good
Morning Heartache. Play the part. Shake
your head, smile a bit, for a while, and when it all
seems too much, a tear, a touch. Oh
Lester's sax! Throw your head back, purl the words,
pearl the words, swirl the words, give the world the words.
Left with no choice, your burdened voice,
your needled arm, your dark-eyed charm. "Strange fruit
hangin' from poplar trees..." "Use the alley door,
if you please!"

LESSONS

At the same age he learned to sight-read
music he began watching for his
father to come home. His father's feet
would ascend the stairs like notes of a scale
on a staff. Ear-trained, he would listen
for the door to slam, hoping to hear
perfect intervals of footsteps, wincing
at sharps, at flats. He took his cues from
his mother as she conducted with
glances, quick nods—as she kept their little
duo always in harmony, no matter
how dissonant the opening chords
of his father's homecoming cadenza.

THE BALTIMORE CATECHISM:
"Who Made The World?"

He is plucked daily from his seat.
His pinched cheek is pulled upward
by a catechist's hand
that smells of cigar smoke.
He remains placid as bare walls.
"God made the world" is beyond him.
He wouldn't know who made the world
if God's very thumb and forefinger
were twisting the side of his face.
Neither does he know
"God is the Creator of heaven and earth,
and of all things."
He does know
that he must offer up his hand
to the yardstick each time
a Catechism question hovers,
unanswered,
in the hollow classroom.
He does not remember
"Man is a creature composed of body and soul,
and made to the image and likeness of God."
His pain is measured in inches.
His palm, repeatedly smitten,
turns ruddy as his cheek,
and he could never guess
"This likeness is chiefly in the soul."

James Benger

RUFUS

There were buckets of broken faucets,
a sink that drained to nowhere,
old bedframes and hobby horses
crammed up in the rafters.

The place was cold and wet and
smelled like last year sealed in a
box to grow mold and discomfort.
Plastic organization totes filled with
random mismatched items.
I sifted through all the stuff, looking
for anything of use to me:
practical or sentimental.
I didn't find much.

Staring at the back wall, the
broken window looking out
to the fallen greenhouse, I felt something
nearly as cold and wet as that
garage. It was nuzzling my hand.

I looked down and saw Rufus, the
pit bull my brother had bought years earlier,
only to turn him loose, and cut town, unofficially
dubbing Rufus the neighborhood stray.

The dog looked at me with hungry recognition.
I fished in my pocket and found the
granola bar I'd been saving for lunch.
I unwrapped it and placed it in
Rufus' eager jaws.
I could see the fleas jumping on his
head while he chewed.

HE LIKE NOTHING

He sat in that old recliner
like it was nothing,
like nothing had happened,
like we didn't know,
couldn't comprehend,
too young to have memories that
stretched back far enough to
incriminate him in our eyes.

He sat in that old recliner,
cigarette ash crawling closer to
his purple knuckles,
yellow nicotine fingernails.
He told stories and laughed,
high, menacing and perverse.
We didn't laugh, took our all to
force cordial, child half-smiles.
With him sitting in that old recliner,
our willful expressions
taught us to lie.

As he sat in that old recliner,
the cigarette burned down with the clock.
He lit another,
hellfire between his cracked lips.

It would never end,
never end.
We were right.
A quarter-century in the ground,
he's still sitting in that old recliner,
telling those stories,
smoking those cigarettes
like nothing had happened.

REACH DOWN

If you came upon me
lying there,
helpless and
completely unaware,
would you offer your hand?

Would you find it in yourself
to forget all the fights,
and ignore all the hurt,
and maybe even
forgo all the pointless pity,
and simply reach down
and pull me up?

Would you do it
with no words?
At a time like that,
nothing needs to be spoken.
We've both always known that.
Would we walk off together,
me leaning on you,
no different than ever, really,
the strong leading the weak,
story of the world.

I won't ask what would be
at the end of that road
we would be hobbling down.
Maybe there'd be no end.
A guy can dream.

FREEDOM RUN

Sometimes we all want to escape.
To just run.
There's a freedom in the roads.
Our predecessors found it in the rails.
An openness,
an acceptance.
We crave it.
An obligation to nothing and no one
but ourselves.
Sure, it would be lonely,
perhaps even empty,
but it would be yours.

Of course, that's not our lot.
We could've had it,
and we chose differently.
Sometimes that freedom calls,
but we've chosen a greater freedom,
one that doesn't require us to run.

GRATEFUL

I walked in on you
finishing up.
You'd be at it a while;
it was painted all over
your face,
all runny and smeared.

It's always awkward to
stumble into those situations,
not sure what to do,
to offer comfort,
or encouragement,
or pretend I saw nothing?

Every time it seems different.
But you were there,
and I was there.
I sat down beside you
on the floor, and I
draped an arm around you.

Annette Billings

NOW WHAT?

Hate has opened its gaping maw
to ingest rhetoric by shovelfuls,
not stopping to chew
what began as our amusement.

Sound bytes, formerly merely irritating,
have festered and shown true selves
on channels switched too late to stop pus
from pouring from what used to be integrity.

Beyond infected,
we are grossly abscessed,
run-through with widespread intolerance,
edematous with pockets of division.

Words, once thought harmless
have morphed to intentional ill will
before our somnolent eyes
and we wonder why contempt spews so freely
from the very platform we allowed it to build.

To label him entertainment
was an irresponsible misnomer
and not a synonym for the "Bully!"
he has always been.

Now what?

Wayne Courtois

CORIOLIS

Fifty years ago, swept up in a life
I tried to care for—rules stringent,
pleasures few—I didn't, as the
song says, know about you. I lived
in the hardscrabble North, while

you lived down the crooked road,
in the bloody Southern Hemisphere,
where water swirled down the drain
clockwise. I couldn't help when
you were bullied and so alone.

Nor was I with you at the theater
in Quito where an old Mexican
horror film scared you to pieces. While
your older brother stayed glued to the screen,
you took refuge beyond the back

row, hiding behind a musty curtain.
You parted it enough to peek now
and then through thick glasses,
nervous left hand smoothing a
cowlick as the black-and-white

nightmare drained the blood from your
face. It was the catacombs, and the
bones had come to life, shrieking
in terror. Even an infant stirred,
a hole in its skull crying for mama.

GIMME YOUR LUNCH MONEY/Wayne Courtois

Scratches and static in the old film
added to the horror, as if it
weren't meant to be seen. And
you made a choice. In the gloom
and dust of that theater, the

Spanish dialogue crackling in your
ears, you chose…not to. Not to
give in, not to horror. If you
had to hide, or look away, or
deny what was happening, you

would. You chose survival over
torment, the willingness to let
the curtain fall. Meanwhile, in
the Northern Hemisphere, where
water swirled down the drain

counterclockwise, I stood in
a six-foot snowdrift, waiting
for the school bus. Fat kid in
a parka, watch cap pulled over
my ears, snow blowing in my face.

I wasn't sure, when the bus
shouldered through the gloom, it
was really there, till it creaked and
sighed to a stop. I knocked my
numb feet against the door to clear

snow from my boots. My glasses
steamed up, snowflakes melted from
my eyebrows and eyelashes. The
bus lurched, I swung into a cold
plastic seat. How long till I could

feel my toes? One long ride past
many fields and a few houses
later, we reached the school. I
struggled down the path to the
gate, placing my boots in bootprints

that went before. I didn't expect to
stay upright for long. Sure enough,
a push from behind landed me in a
snowbank. Hands pulled my hood back,
shoveled snow down my neck. I'd

be wet and cold all day, my feet
thawing out, then freezing again
at recess. You could say I was numb
from the neck up as well. Eyes lowered,
voice squeaking, I never took the

practical path, choosing between
sanity and horror. My winter went
on forever, while you fought the good
fight, sweating out the days when
bullies had their ways and the

future looked grim. Perhaps we
were connected even then, tears
swirling down our faces in
different directions, meeting in
the middle. Turns out that swirling

thing is a myth—Coriolis doesn't
care about our personal drainage.
It has more important things to do,
far above our heads, like making
cyclones. Here's what matters:

turning in our separate spirals we
found each other, chose survival
over agony, and vanquished
the horror of our early years,
the difference in hemisphere.

Pat Daneman

BOYS WHO CUT THE LEGS OFF BOX TURTLES

You're sure these are the same two who smash
jack-o-lanterns up and down the street and name
your brother Four-Eyes and pinch your nipples
on the school bus, who steal baseball cards
kids have clothes-pinned to their bicycle spokes
and call them fairies when they cry. They come
at night over the fence into your backyard

to the pen with foil pie tins spilling lettuce,
the cement pool you helped your father pour
and shape where you like to wash the turtles' shells
because the water makes the orange markings
shine like the lid of your grandmother's jewelry box.
One leg off each of the babies. Both
hind legs off big Bo, which is the name

you'd give a dog if you had one. That morning
you go out to see how they are doing
with the lettuce and find them—beaks opening,
closing in panic that you do not understand
until you pick Bo up and see only his front legs
treading air. Your father promises if you take them
back to the woods where you caught them, new legs

GIMME YOUR LUNCH MONEY / Pat Daneman

will grow, so you do. You leave them under the bushes
near the pond, watch for awhile as they do not move.
The next time you see those boys—who after
high school will be sent to Vietnam—you shoot them
your most unflinching evil eye, wish them missing
limbs and nightmares to help them think about
what they have done.

Dennis Etzel, Jr.

FROM *ROBINSON MIDDLE SHAM*

wrestling team photo
I thought there were only bullies
in the group kind-hearted boys
hidden as everyone
had to talk about fight club
mention Brownback here
now and his lackey comes charging in
demanding the speech be halted
the teacher silenced
as children watch bullies
remain bullies

CLEANING THE FLAT GRILL

I scrape the carbon off of the flat grill,
as another member from the kitchen
is off—let go—after the manager
yells at him, tells him to mop the back room
before leaving. The grill scraper is sharp—
takes off the brown ashes. The manager
jokes with me about something, as a way
to let the boy know he is not wanted.

I push down hard to get the residue
off the metal, wishing for smooth silver
again. The manager turns his back on
that young man he laughs at. I do my best—
to nod, smile, continue to scrape away
any hope for this surface to be clean.

Gu Jieming Gulley

I COULD TELL HE WAS TRYING TO SING

I could tell he was trying to sing.
His mom told me he used to . . . a lot,
"until he got annoying," she said,
and I imagined her . . . remembering,
wishing he was annoyingly singing again
instead of the grunts that made up his
full vocal repertoire since his step-dad
locked him in the upstairs closet and
set the house on fire, and his mom,
having no other options, threw him
out of the window, and he landed face
down on the sidewalk . . . age 8.
But still, 10 years later,
I could tell he was trying to sing.

Tina Hacker

A JEWISH GIRL PONDERS SKIN

Amanda says I'm shrouded
head to toe in Original Sin.
She tells me I have to get rid of it.
I imagine a second skin
of original sin. Maybe like
my flannel nightgowns,
smooth, warm, long sleeved.
Amanda tries to dissolve it,
imitating Dorothy in Oz.
She aims her water pistol
at my face muttering a prayer.
No Baptism here.
Satan is hovering near, she says
when I appear unchanged.

NOT A CRIME

The principal took the second graders
down to the school basement to view
a shower stall. Like a prison warden
showing an isolation cell to murderers,
he gave a lecture, his voice snapping,
words landing like the lash of a whip.
He ordered them to use the stall
if they didn't bathe at home.
The children eyed each other.
More than a few raised their noses
hoping to inhale evidence. All lived
in small flats. Some were poor,
others barely middle class,
several recent immigrants
sharing rooms with other families.
No one had a second bathroom.
Many kids fought World War Bath
each night. The principal's threat
hung over them ready to strike.
One girl, a new student, squirmed
more than the others.
Is he talking about me?

DINNER OUT

She read the menu items aloud.
Her voice didn't have to carry far,
just across a small table.
After reciting her choice of entree,
she paused, waiting for a response,
a comment from him,
but received a shrug, the faintest of shrugs,
one that would not bestow
a grace of energy.
And when the waiter arrived,
he relayed her choice,
emphasizing the words on the menu
she had omitted.
He picked up his fork and wiped
each tine carefully,
then the knife, then the spoon.
Studying each of his movements,
she pursed her lips tightly,
but a scream below hearing
made its way to her eyes
and carried across the table.
Armored against such assaults,
his eyes did not answer.
He stared behind her, above her,
then leaned back, his chest falling into his spine,
a retreat before a familiar enemy.
She folded into herself
like the napkin crumpled in her hand.

Robert Haynes

SHE WHO HAD NOTHING TO LOSE

You can call it anything. But when it began,
each day must have been a little death, a practice
for the big one that would not hurry.

I wonder if she remembers me as I do her.
If everywhere she goes people are together,
& she is the one who binds them?

I did not want to know her or anyone like her.
If we spoke or touched, disease might rub off on me.

But I had to dance with her once in Social Hour.
She curtsied and took my hand, her tumors
in my palm. My heart rattled like an earthquake
as I squinted into her scars. Everywhere we went,

my friends & I told each other how awful it was
and dreamed we sneaked at night into her bedroom
like a mob in a movie and lynched her up.

What a pink throat it was.
What prayers it must have held.

A MAN THAT MAD DON'T FAN HIMSELF

How it must have been.
The night cool for a change: a thin
sheet over them, and the black metal fan
oscillating an obstinate no....

how the 19-year-old had opened
her legs for the first time, daydreaming

about a farmer who swings
his flat-nosed shovel just the right way
over his shoulder. He takes fists full of water
right out of the cistern,
rubs the wet hands through his hair.

She inhales the soft clods of earth,
digs into the folds of his overalls...
She just wants to stop

listening to what the fan says, to stop
caring if it's sanctuary or grave . . .
the dirt or the way he beats
his path in and out of here, belching
good feelings gone wrong.

Even the chickens won't argue that.

All she has in mind
is his fist, drawn back and dripping.

FORCE OF THE SONOGRAM

Sight may first stir the itching
possibility to include a torso
in which the blur on the screen is
drawn by pixels and stretched
tight as slats in venetian blinds.

A thought awakens eyelashes
to slim verticals of light, to the infected
mattress in the alleyway.
The blur might be wings lifting
a baby's head, or it could be an angel,

or mother of an angel.
Nonetheless, another likelihood awaits
that tells you time and again

that someone else's God
by his own choosing loves you—
or not—as the case may be.

Melissa Fite Johnson

HIGH SCHOOL PEP BAND

My flute part never sounded like the song
on its own. When I practiced,
my brother poked his head in my room,
asked if I had any idea what the hell I was doing.
But with the band, the flutes' voices
soared higher than even the trumpets'
bold balloon squeaks.

The trumpets—and indeed the trombones,
saxes, tubas, even clarinets—
none of them questioned our worth.
We had each other's backs. We had to.

At the basketball games, we held a kind of
nerd power. No one said much
to us in classes or the halls, but they
loved us at games. They yelled
the words to every song. Together we lifted
those boys, high as the cheerleaders
somersaulting into the air. We were
part of something on those nights.
We were really in high school.

On Mondays we were back to visitor status,
stepping aside to let a row of letter jackets pass.

ON RAY RICE

> *Comments on the YouTube video defending
> the NFL athlete knocking out his fiancée in an elevator*

Dumb bitch started it. Cunt
ruined his career. Too bad
he didn't break her fucking jaw off.
Act like a man, try and hit one,
get treated like a man. This is what
equality looks like. Girls
are as much of a threat
as guys. She slapped him first.
She's the aggressor. What the fuck
do you see? A man beating
his woman? He defended himself
against a human being with
the potential to hurt him.
All those white feminists need to
shut the fuck up. Period. This is
what equality looks like. It probably
wasn't his intention to knock her out,
but shit happens. She should've
thought of that before assaulting
an NFL player. A woman
deserves equal rights.
She has to take responsibility
for her actions. She had it coming.
This is what equality looks like.

NINETEEN

Sick of him saying
how much prettier I'd be
with a flat stomach, I sign up
for body toning class.
There, a girl is missing
a hand. She duct tapes her
almost fist to a free
weight when it's time
to work our biceps.
I wonder sometimes
if she has a boyfriend and
what he must say to her.

HALLOWEEN 2014

On the news, this eight-year-old's costume:

White boy in black face,
Rice jersey, giddily drags
a doll by her hair.

I imagine this boy with his parents.
On the couch, their faces flicker shadows
from Dad's laptop. They absorb
the NFL highlight, dismiss the black
couple's domestic dispute as drunk,
savage. At the mall, Mom finds the jersey,
shakes her head, stifles a laugh. Dad nods, holds it
against their son, who growls and bites the air.

We all witnessed the same footage—the man
hoisting the woman across the open
elevator's threshold, dumping her
limp body on the ground,
a parody of the wedding night tradition.

Gary Lechliter

THEM FOLKS

We sometimes wander the landscapes
of those we badge as odd or strange,
where the bell curve flattens to lines
outside the norm, like the judge
pacing his backyard and the girl
who won't step outside her home.

Different ones scare us: The boy who's lonely
and gay and can't marry in Kansas,
the "Hat Woman" standing at the curb
and advising them folks where
salvation's found, who they must serve,
and asks can they spare some change?

There's the man who's afraid of rain,
who finds it hard to make sense
of it all, to hold reason on the dark day,
when he draws the blinds and prays
for drought, while clouds spill
enough rain to cleanse the town.

And it's fear of the strange
that calls the neighborhood bully
to loose his dog to frighten passersby,
the neighbors and the postman,
the sellers of faith and magazines,
because they're different.

SKIDMORE

A pall from the coffin seems
to linger here, even after thirty-five years.
Bricks hold a trace of it—with the image
of the nameless face, the hero
who rid the town of a bully
so vile that even the local sheriff
had no office when called for.

When it's a long time between beers
and piss, the townsfolk go on
as they must with farming
and drug stores, children at the
bus stop, the honored stories of
the bully's kids, ten in all, lost
mothers of forsaken breasts.

And even today, the town's name
calls questions of guilt or relief.
Those who remember walk back
the logic that the needs of many
outweigh the ignorance of one.
That the law's a fluid, pliant thing,
if the end justifies the blood.

INCIDENT AT RIDERS FORD
(Winter, 1967)

More feminine than girls I knew,
he had more verve than the boys.
Quiet and polite, he was easily bullied
by Baptists and Catholics alike.
All the bible-thumpers preached that
different people are doomed.

This is how it was in the Heartland,
for anyone far from the norm.
He wore panties beneath his slacks.
Someone said he was queer.
But the rumor was never vetted.

All that mattered in our town
was to fit in where you could, do your
part, walk like a man and spit snuff,
gaze through cracks in the girl's shower,
say fuck daily just to say it, damn
the Russians, the Chinese, the Jews.

But he would have none of bigotry.
A kind soul with a warm smile,
the FFA boys took him to the river,
de-pants him and left him naked
in darkness that hides stupidity.

When the police found him dazed
and shivering in the street,
he refused to identify the thugs
or press charges, and nothing
was done; they got away with
simian, primordial acts.

Denise Low

MUSIC LESSONS

Fourteen and developed,
I am a morsel trapped
in the music studio.
He never lays a hand on me
but after my wheezy scales
he smirks about blow jobs.

In the Army he liked
whores. Sex, he says,
is rubbing sticks together.
I play "Take Five"
as his fingers drum
the rhythm by my face.

His girlfriend is country,
raw-boned, soft-spoken.
When I'm sixteen
we drive to a jazz concert
in his big gray Chrysler.
Their baby is on the way.

Goldie Manasseh

CIRCUMSTANTIAL BULLY

You ain't pretty.
You're so petty,
You don't deserve a penny.
You should stay home at prom.

Crucially bad I must say.
But have you been to Africa?
Bet you won't stay.
For these you crave amnesia,
We call them compliments.

You'd offer your money,
But hell! They're richer.
They'll give you a bunny,
And buy you prom dresses.
Then, ask for your blood.

They strip off your dignity,
With canes, and blows.
You'll face the penalty,
They'll say with glows,
And taunting stares.

GIMME YOUR LUNCH MONEY / Goldie Manasseh

Wasn't born a wrestler,
But when my demons came,
I couldn't be a dancer.
Oh! I never overcame,
But I lived to tell.

They don't care if you're black.
They just hate that you exist.
All I can say, looking back,
They made a circumstantial bully
Out of me.

Lindsey Martin-Bowen

THE BIG C
to Carl

"I'm cold," your mother says
and quivers. She can't find
comfort in my words. I see
blue veins pucker her hands
and fingers, so I close the door
and leave her lonely condo.
My boots crunch snow,

and winds careen me
while I clomp across the parking lot.
Once, I didn't mind icicles
clutching branches,
crystals of sunlight
creating prisms of white and blue
like scales on a carp diving.

But tonight, they crackle
and become carotids
pointing to a crusty lawn.
Like some bully carousing
on the corner, they wait
for a skinny kid in glasses.
Crouching in shadows,
he's afraid to step across a crack.

JIM MORRISON RESCUES ME

Jim says he won't let me be bullied again.
He floats out of the stereo, takes my hands,
rubs my face, and adds, "We're leaving.
Hiding in your room makes life too heavy."
He lures me into a Chevy rumbling at the curb.
Wind brushes our cheeks while we drive
to the beach. Seaweed and moss scents lift
our fragile spirits. A red sun seems to sear
Jim's curls into fire, while we lie on the sand.

Waves shuttle in cockle shells and oysters.
We hear flamingos click while they
entwine their necks, step to hot rhythms
and morph into pink Hispanic dancers.
Gulls squawk and dip into water.
Here, on this shore, Jim and I lie
away from paparazzi, safe from critics—
except those Shaman voices
reverberating in our brains.

Ronda Miller

AMONG THE WILD PRIMROSE

My white sleeveless tee is dirty,
sand burrs reside in the cruelest
of places, cheeks stained,
dirt tears weave a ragged trail
of sexual abuse.

I remain hidden a long time
after the sun goes down,
hours after my grandparents' car
winds up the gravel road,
makes its way inside the garage
attached to the barn.

My sister's voice rings out
clearly, joyfully, "Roni? Roni,
we're home!"
She left hours before.
Her first prom.
She wears a peach formal
that highlights her delicate,
porcelain skin.

Among the wild primrose and
rattlesnake master I hunker.
I have no words to tell what
happened when my grandfather
called me to sit on his lap.
He told me how ugly
I was as he touched me.

GIMME YOUR LUNCH MONEY / Ronda Miller

I'm turned away from him—
perhaps too ugly to be seen.
I become invisible.

I carry my ugliness throughout
my life. I'm made aware each
time I'm touched by any man.
The police officers I work
with call me Cunt, Dickless
Tracy. They stop by my house
off-duty hours
in uniform.

I carry my sexuality as my value.
I don't wait to be approached.
I offer myself willingly
to complete strangers.
It's what I have.
It's what I know.
Relationships flower
short-lived
as a wild primrose.

BORN TO BULLY

Baby birds burned
as firecrackers crackled,
tadpoles exploded,
kittens tossed from roofs.
It was all a gas,
normal boyish pranks.
Put cinnamon oil
in a baby's eye, let's see
if it makes him blink
or makes him cry!

What kind of demon
does all this? His parents
thought having a son
would bring them bliss.
He's spanked,
he's whipped,
to no avail.
Is it any surprise
he ends in jail?
He steals, he lies,
takes money from sons
and ex wives.
He's a master manipulator,
a gem of disguise.

EVERY THING THEY HAD

Faces I love sit in silence.
Personalities once strong,
outspoken, defined, now
afraid to speak their minds.
Heads down, ashamed,
as if they've done
something wrong.
Control taken
by a signed affidavit
that gives Power of Attorney
over their lives.
An only son smiles, says,
"Do you trust me, Dad?"
The paper is pushed across
the table as is the diagnosis
of terminal cancer.
A wave goodbye and he's gone.
Gotta catch a flight
to his busy life.
My uncle sits in silence,
cries, the first I've seen it.
Bullying comes in many forms.
Bully on you. Bully on me
for I am silenced too;
in shock about how quickly
we write off those who
spent their entire lives
giving
every thing.

Caryn Mirriam-Goldberg

HAPPINESS

I knew happiness in one continuous motion
the moment the midwife held up a knife and cut me,
everything shining and breaking. There, pressing
against the window, the cottonwoods that would frame
your childhood, rushing toward us in leaf and wind.

In the dark branches skinned white and peeling
I was just like you, clanging all over inside.
"What's wrong with you, you stupid schmuck-head?"
my father would ask. And my mother, "Remember
to try to make friends." I was your age, Daniel,
friendless, so they took me in the taxi
past the singular birches to see my first shrink, trembling
that the first child didn't understand something vital
about how to glance at the world.

What did I need with the world when I had the tree?
Its legs mined the earth for water,
the very book of happiness, opening
up the spine of each rounding leaf.
Then the wind that would not control itself—
always a miracle, a miracle
to watch no matter how long I waited
from my seven-year-old window,
all the bruises on my arms and legs solitary,
the belt my father used for this
demilitarized on the floor. I was actually happy
and nothing could undo that.

WHAT I COULD TELL

I could name all the pieces of violence—
the kick or slap, the friendly punch.
"Say it again," the therapist says.
I remember this later, lying in the bathtub
watching my arms and legs float in water, so normal.
Do you see how contained I am? How calm
a poem, as if I were writing about
tree limbs in winter covered in ice. Delicate.
Connected to the glass trunk, bone to bone.

I startle awake. Someone behind me. Reflexes
not everyone has anymore or ever.
But that was another time, weighted in
the cells of skin. Smoke in the vein of the bone.
Does it matter that the shelf of sky was blue,
that there was heat right where
the fist imprinted itself on my leg?
Did it happen like a shovel edge into roots,
someone watching, hands around my neck
before I could speak, and I'm dying
all over again?

There was a room with no air, a cringing
inward, the iris already broken from its bulb.
There was a bathtub with a girl covered
in bruises, the door locked hopefully.

She was tired, so tired
she couldn't stay awake
to tell me what really happened.

Eve Ott

ONCE UPON A TIME

Model it, Baby, model it, he said.

Holding the long skirt
of my new nightie
and arching one arm
above my head
I turned
on tip-toe
before my aunt and uncle.

He threw his head back and roared
which stopped me in my tracks.
I must have done it wrong.

But then, as Auntie went to the kitchen,
he swept me up in his arms
and carried me upstairs,
lifted my pretty new nightie,
sat me in his lap,
unzipped,
and began my bedtime story.

PEDAL HARDER

The new boyfriend is making his confessions,
a sign he is serious, serious, about them.
Not just drugs, no,
theft, domestic violence,
knowledge of explosives,
tested, successfully.

He who seemed so sweet,
so good to her fatherless child,
also so eager to please, so needy,
which actually she did see as red flags.
Now there's progress.

I'm not the person I used to be,
he says.

I shudder.
Know he probably wishes
but also know Her Kind of Guy,
back again.

I wonder if it's just me, she says,
so untrusting, so suspicious because of—

Is he out? I ask.
Yes, but circling.

Of course.
But months rather than years this time.

I'm here, I say.
I can be there, if you want.

Usually we email or she texts.
A phone call is serious.

When we hang up,
on our traditional I-love-yous,
(and, you know what?
sometimes traditional's all you've got.
And sometimes it is totally sincere),

I look out my window
close to KC metro
and see a little knobby-kneed girl
wobbling around our little triangle
with the red maple in the middle
in her bright pink T
on her brand new bike,

and I whisper:
Peddle harder, darling,
harder, harder.

MY BULLY

His name was Gordon.
I lived in the middle of the street,
he lived on the corner
of the street we all walked to school.
Groups of children, K-8,
meeting up at corners
where "Uncle Sam Needs You" posters hung,

GIMME YOUR LUNCH MONEY / Eve Ott

along with "Loose Lips Sink a Ship,"
kids on the East Coast of the U.S.
growing up behind black-out curtains
and hooded headlights
hearing air raid sirens
which sent us to huddle
next to the walls in the school basement,
but who, nonetheless walked to school
where Gordon, a year older than me, lurked
and tormented me from kindergarten through 3rd grade,
grabbed my hat or my mittens,
and dangling them just out of reach,
rubbed my face in the rough, gray snow
pushed by the plow to the side of the street.
He threw my paper with the gold star to March winds,
all the while laughing, laughing,
until 3rd grade
when I took a growth spurt
while he stayed pale and slight.
I chased him home,
wrestled him to the ground,
straddled his chest,
and pummeled him
until his mother came out
and shouted me home.
There I suffered the two days
he did not go to school,
terrified that I had seriously injured him,
or worse, enacted the murder in my heart that day.
Gordon did return to school.
Our eyes neither met nor did we speak
as I followed him all the way through high school.
Years later, I learned what the adult neighbors knew,
that Gordon's father had a strict order
of punishments for infractions,
from a slap, to a back-handed slap, to the switch,
to the paddle, to the belt, to the belt buckle,

all administered in the dark, dank basement
of their little house. No one reported such things
back then when children were their parents.'
More years later, I learned that Gordon spent years
in college to become a psychiatrist,
which at first caused me to shudder.
Then, I imagined that through his studies
Gordon had come to understand himself
and his father, and had led many, many others
from that dark space of lonely impotence
to the light of compassion and community.
Gordon was a childhood bully, yes,
but he was my bully.
I wish him well.

Shawn Pavey

PAYING UP

You never had a chance, Fat Boy,
with your love of books and talent for music,
glasses thick as Coke-bottle bottoms,
lack of eye-hand coordination,
and general inability at all things athletic.

Sure, there were friends, but they never
seemed to be around when
the Houston brothers roamed
small town streets looking for an easy target
to make themselves feel better
about the beatings they took at home.

Dan Pohl

EIGHTEEN MOVES TO CHECKMATE

As a new kid
Untethered to one town
I followed my father's life
Construction of dams and roads
That ran across Kansas
I-70, Ellis to Leavenworth
Took eight years, and
With each move
I would evaporate as smoke does
Like I was never there
So why make friends
Just to leave them
All that time and energy
To cry goodbye
Isolated
A Russian novelist
Self-caged in a small upper room
With a writer's fear
To fill eight-hundred blank pages
Yet wolves know the smell
Of prey's blood
And I cannot find enough wine
To clear my invisible ledger
That holds little profit
Of friendships
Adding the compound interest
Of villains like in Dicken's novels
Tacked to memory

GIMME YOUR LUNCH MONEY / Dan Pohl

Unable to erase their derisions
That began at their city limits
Who made newcomers feel
Like a Peanuts character
Alone in the outfield
Worried by their words
And often Goliaths fought my David
Never knowing
Like they did
What was fair
What was right
Asking where the good kids hid
Wondering why they could not find me
From the first or second moment
There among the rat bastards
Who stole their fathers' cigarettes
Drank their mothers' liqueur
And me
Feeling homesick
For someone gentle.

DRONES
for Roy Beckemeyer

Like Harley riders
They insist on that thunderous din
From their bikes
Knowing full well they have a choice
Of quiet mufflers.
Like cigarette smoke
Wafting over to my dinner table
Unsolicited
Unasked for
(Sure, blow some more smoke
In my face, you twit)
Years ago
Before the bullied rose up
By economic boycott
Voting with our feet
Signing petitions for the good food

Drones
Still need to fly quietly
But does the property line
Of my house rise into altitude
I side
With the guy with the shot gun
If they cross the line
When I sunbathe semi-naked
I request no drones overhead

GIMME YOUR LUNCH MONEY / Dan Pohl

Therefore
If I have now placed
That unsettling image
In your mind without your permission
Have I not imposed myself
Without asking permission
To do so?

FOR THOSE WHO CAN RELATE

Yeah, to fight an evil bully, is it true
I must become one, giving myself
Permission to break my governor
That which stops my hand, to push
Him from top the monkey bars for
Relief from shoves and names
I remember or to turn with a sharp
Pencil, driving it deep for the foot
That tapped my desk chair in fifth
Grade or to super glue a high school
Locker handle for not giving the SOB
Extra towels after PE class to warrant
A beating after school, always with
No teacher or adult around? Yeah
I can, to stop the terrorists, but there
Is always another, another, another
And I found in so doing that I can
Never quite regain what I once was—
A good kid.

FIFTIES TOURISTS

Of our nameless generation
Too early for Vietnam, too
Late to protest war, the kids
In Keds sneakers had a fair
Share of accidents, fender
Benders, hits that left scars
So we chowed down to keep
Our machines moving on a
Lonely road, filled with pothole
Bullies. We slid around them
With our laces tied and shirts
Tucked in, the best we could
Collecting enough salvaged parts
To heal our hides, alive, sane
But could not find enough beer
To erase images in mind of our
Distant history. Yet we remain.

WHY THE DRAMA OF THE SOCIALLY PUZZLED

> "Mean as a man who tells his children
> that Santa Claus is dead."
> —Anonymous

Mean as a bully stripping wallpaper
From the inner room of the soul, its
Spirit dispirited, the cold unneeded
In the center of social demolition
It takes only derision, snobbish in
Tone when said out of mouth with
No lock on self-control. Then, to leave,
A friend walks away, no explanation
Evil as good, misunderstanding, little
Said to explain what's wrong by a
Snake, villain, bitter people who do
Not speak to know the missing piece.

Jeanette Powers

FAMILY TRADITION

You were beaten until
your glasses and teeth broke
you were ignored and over-
worked, touched by your step-father
you were deaf till five
you were raped by every step-father
for years. You were taught
god was salvation

you were told you were the messiah
you were told you were the devil
you were told your opinion didn't matter
to shut up and get out
that you were a worthless little shit
that you had no brains no future no guts no sense,
and in the meantime
your father drank himself
into oblivion and violence
your mother was blind.

The parents who made you
try to kill you as surely
it's the family tradition
the father who kicked you
the mother who called you disgusting
miserablefilthyidiotlittleassholecunt
who blamed you for their lives
and so beat you, taunted you
allowed you to be damaged.

GIMME YOUR LUNCH MONEY/Jeanette Powers

And we?
artists because we have to be
else we'd be out there as missionaries
for the system we inherited
fathers beating, mothers letting
stepfathers raping, mothers being jealous
mothers' killing words, fathers being gone
mothers and fathers be damned.

I'll be your father, you be mine
we'll fuck and make a mother to beat them all.
She will stride big and strong in blue jeans
and a baseball t-shirt that says "Athena"
stout-legged and gorgeous breasts
she has milk enough for all of us
and honey to follow
her braids are long as Rapunzel's
salvation and we swing through
the mountains of her capacity to love
as though we were the wind
and her arms were the air.

She is a destroyer of destroyers
our Mamma-Shiva
our Matron Saint
the one we should have had.

Kevin Rabas

RING-CUT

Spindly wore rings on his fists,
big ones, sharp ones, the grooves
blood-ringed, blood-thick, gems
red-speckled. When Spindly came in
from black top, playground,
someone's face bloomed red,
ring-cut, knuckle-cut, sunk
by Spindly's quick, thick fists.

Carl Rhoden

MIGUEL'S STORY

In here,
the walls have teeth.
They are always hungry.

When a man screams,
it is because
the walls are eating him.

The priest was eaten
yesterday.
He did not scream.

If a man does not scream,
the walls are angry
and do not eat him quickly.

The priest was eaten
very slowly.
I think God made them

take all day.
No one else
was eaten.

GUNS BEER LIQUOR AMMO ICE

Stop cryin' you little baby.
Are you a boy or a girl?
Your mother's not comin'.
Do you know who your father is?
Say, what color are you?
Where'd you get those ears, fatty?
Pigeon-toed freak four-eyes . . .
you can't hang with us.
You can't eat with us.
Go to the back of the bus.
You're ugly. What's that smell?
Go play with your dolls. Go
play with yourself. You killed
Jesus, you creep! What'll we
Do with you? Go back
Where you came from. Stop
takin' up space freeloader!
You're not even American.

WHERE DID THE BODY COME FROM?

(photograph, El Salvador, 1981)

That should be the title
of this picture—
six children stopped

on a sidewalk
to stare at the naked man
face down in the curb.

It's morning.
Dressed in school uniforms,
they're on their way

to learn.

SHE STILL CANNOT SPEAK

If I tell you what
they did, if I
describe in detail
who they were
and their number,
why it was done,
what they used,
where they used it
on her, how she
was left, where
she was left,
for how long and
what it was
that found her—
maybe you should
sit.

TO SEE AN ELEPHANT CRY

Researchers wire her with monitors.
Probing her crown, trunk, and ears,
electroscopes bring her tears. A cage
atop her back pokes her spine, wrecking it,
as they search this elephant's dreams
to glean hidden rhythms, secrets
she won't share about living a long life.

—Lindsey Martin-Bowen

Ki Russell

BATH

After Langston Hughes

The calm,
cool face of the river
asked me for a kiss

and it sucks the air
out of my lungs
replaces it with acid
eyes shut tight
like you told me
they should be when you kissed my
nine-year-old lips
with your forty-year-old ones.
my lungs
burn with water

your hand print rinses off.

THE ANTLER WOMAN RESPONDS

After Mark Doty

On misty-gray, not-dark, not-light days
I feel bone sprout from my temples.
I try to catch a glimpse in store windows.

I should keep my eyes on the ground
instead of stepping out of forwardness.
But my allegiance is not to permanent forms.

Plain clothes hide hooves and haunches,
the elongated grammar of muscle,
and me without a trench coat.

I am the respiration of the grass
and my animal alphabet
fails on a regular basis.

Years from now on a tonal night
my feet will evaporate into cloud
and my antlers will twine with stardust.

For now I am less anatomy
than a storm, a glittering, gathering mass,
an antlered woman dodging traffic.

INFATUECTOMY

wind slices
my skin
a scalpel
opening me
to remove
the parasite
that slid
into my ear
when you said
my name

Ralph Seligman-Courtois

TABLE TENNIS TOURNAMENT

High school gymnasium,
Ten ping-pong tables clacking
As players swing back and forth
To score the winning point.

One ball flies beyond the table
Bouncing gingerly away from me.
I chase after it as a good spectator would,
Stop it in mid-roll, crush it underfoot.

Bold and brutish boy barrages me.
"How can you be so stupid!
You must replace it, ASAP!
No later than tomorrow!"

On my way home I stop by a store.
They only sell them by the dozen.
I buy them, no other choice.
Hoping to undo the damage done.

I give the box to the brutish boy.
He returns a look of disgust.
"These are the cheapest kind.
And the tournament is over, anyway."

EROSION

I know it's just a scrape,
A little bruise that will fade.

I know it's just a little taunt
That will haunt me late at night.

I know it's just a joke,
One that even I might laugh at.

I know it was a playful shove
That caught me unawares.

You remind me each time
As I pour my heart to you,

Of the horrible events
That happened to you.

I must be strong, you say,
Such things are but small.

But to a wall already crumbling
Each brick placed on top

Does not strengthen, but instead,
Burdens it and adds more weight,

Making it harder to bear
And adding to the wear and tear,

To an ego already weak
Nearing the breaking point,

To go ahead and soothe my pain,
But leave the rest for other times,

When I am strong and confident,
To offer comfort back to you.

Then we can lean on each other
And strengthen together.

CLOVER SO FRAGRANT

Clover so fragrant.
Not as sweet smelling when your
Face is pushed ground-ward.

TO THE RESCUE

I saw them standing there
All alone in the crowd,
Matthew, Torgei, Ken, and Stephen.

New kids in my school
Not knowing anyone
Not knowing where to go.

I introduce myself
In my limited English
In my broken German.

"I do not speak Norwegian,"
I explain to Torgei, yet
We muddle through anyhow.

They feel I've rescued them
From loneliness and
Taught them the ropes.

They do not realize that
While being guided by me,
I was the one needing rescuing.

BULLY VS. ALLY

It hurts!
—Baby!

It hurts!
—Relax!

I won't!
—Lazy!

I won't!
—What's wrong?

I'm scared!
—Pussy!

I'm scared!
—Hold on!

Don't make me!
—Wuss!

Don't make me!
—Try it like this!

I can't do it!
—Chicken!

I can't do it!
—Tell me why.

Tyler Sheldon

GROWING UP FREE

Riding the void between streetlights,
the neighborhood bully
squats like a fist in the dark,
waiting to knuckle down
on spectacled skinnies
who begin to know better
a little too late, who dance
through those midnight lights
and are caught on the chin
by America.

Alarie Tennille

SHE DOESN'T HAVE TO CALL ME A BITCH

Everything about her
shouts it—the red face, bared
teeth, the way she charges
like a shrieking hyena. Ignoring
the older man beside me, she singles
me out for the kill. "YOU
are destroying the family!"
she screams. Hoisting a sweaty
baby like a trophy, she sputters,
"MY daughter is going to be a LADY!"

I sit at an outdoor table, spread
with N.O.W. pamphlets and petitions
for the Equal Rights Amendment.
I look her in the eye, say nothing,
become a wall that her words
bounce off. She turns on her heel,
huffs away.

The silence sizzles.

SUMMER 1970, THE UNIVERSITY OF VIRGINIA OPENS TO WOMEN IN THE FALL

Mama calls me a pioneer. I call
me a student—tagging along
after my older brother like always,
ignoring his taunts. You can't
come here. Somehow I knew
I would.

At thirteen, I fell in love
with Thomas Jefferson's Rotunda
and vistas of the Blue Ridge.
I'm not trying to make history,
just taking my place in it.

Brave? No, timid and half-blind.
Every stranger and new school
scares me. That's life.
I don't know I'll need extra
courage. That will come later.

Maryfrances Wagner

MENDING LEROY'S SWEATER IN COMPOSITION

Leroy swaggers into my class without books
or pen, jams hands into his pockets, face
partly hidden under his black hoodie.
He stares at his desk after all questions.

Students step around him and his gym bag
to trade papers. They have always kept
their distance. His fight last weekend
after the football game gave them proof.

He waits for the principal to suspend him.
He'll be gone five school days for the fight
behind the stadium, blood scrubbed clean
now from asphalt, bats, and knuckles.

A row of stitches jags across his eyebrow.
He rocks in his seat, glares. Heads bowed,
students write comments on rough drafts.
The register hisses. It is snowing.

I look up. Leroy opens his hoodie to show me
the rip in his sweater, sets a button on my desk.
We stare at each other. I rummage for a needle,
point to the window where light is best.

The ground outside is covered and unmarred by tracks.
I pin the rip along the seam near his waist, think
of how to situate myself, the angle so low. He
rests a hand on my arm. I kneel beside him and sew.

KASTAVAS PUTS IT ON THE LINE

In my writing class, Brian nudges Kastavas awake,
Sleep at night, Dude. Kastavas jolts up from
a pool of drool. *Fuck you, Skater! Dude, I work late.*
The students snap their faces left, stare at Kastavas.

I lean on one foot, then the other, chew my cheek,
tap a pencil, dip into the drawer for a Write Up.
Yesterday, Kastavas handed me two sonnets and an essay.
I know how he lives. I know about his father.

He smears an inked heart on his desk.
You know the rules, I say and slap the Write Up form
in front of him. *I'll see you after class.*
He slumps across the room to sharpen a pencil.

I collect student journals. Kastavas presses
so hard in his that he leaves a ghost copy
on the page behind it. I read it like a Watermark.

Diane Wahto

THE YELLOW DRESS

She went to the basement where they kept
tools, kids' toys, where they hunkered down
when the tornado blew over the spring before,
hit the Burger King on the highway. She thought
he would not think to look there for her, given
his state so late at night. When she heard
his steps on the stairs, she knew.

He ripped her yellow dress, the dress the color
of spring flowers, the dress with the white
stripe down the front that neatly defined
her body, saying as he tore it at the seams
that he had always hated that dress on her.
He dragged her up the basement steps,
up the carpeted stairs to the bedroom, the kids
awake by now, hearing the sounds of struggle,
the sounds of the bed as he dragged her to it,
as he tore off her white underpants, her bra,
as he climbed on top, filled her body with his spite.
The next time, it was winter. The oldest son ran
barefoot across the street to tell the neighbors
to call the police. They came, their blue uniforms
impeccable, their guns holstered in shiny leather.
They told her she and the kids had to leave.
He sat on the carpeted stairs, his face a mask
of innocence and hurt pride.
She couldn't find her other shoe.

WATCHING *APOCALYPSE NOW* WITH MY FRIEND DAVE

This is the third time I've seen it,
the second time with Dave. Why
I torture myself with these scenes,
now so familiar, still full of horror,
I will never know. We sit on the floor,
drinks in hand, pillows at our back,
talk as familiar scenes roll past us.
"Ride of the Valkyries" fills the room
with the whap-whap of helicopters
in the background. Death falls
from placid skies, from hidden
jungle perils, from guns, least
expected by villagers on a once
peaceful day. Nightmare nights,
a bridge alight with color, flares.

Laura Madeline Wiseman

ORIGINAL TROLLS

I decide to search for original trolls. I ask, *Do you want to go?* You mutter about your clubs, the backyard. I say, *I'm going to go, then.* It is a long journey, but I take Melatonin. I take Dramamine. I sleep seventeen hours upon arrival. In a Dublin pub called Mr. Toad's with seats like London's Tower, I sit among the drinkers. I let one buy me Irish coffee. He buys each round, each time sitting a little closer, even though the chairs are built into the wall. *I'm looking for original trolls,* I say. He says, *You've come to the right place.* He leads me out, buys me a baguette with cheese, a crystal goblet, a plaid tam. When a chubby street urchin girl begs for a bite, he says, *Bugger off.* I'm charmed by his big hands, the gap between his teeth, his whistle. It's familiar, a melody I can't place. I get into his car. I buy the petrol. He drives into the green hills to where he says the trolls are. Endlessly, he rubs my thigh. Endlessly, I watch for trolls. His touch remind me of yours, something cold. When he stops the car, I search for the door handle to look for trolls, but there aren't handles in his car.

INSIDE THE ROOTED PASSAGE

He tells me, *You're bad,* and leads me toward the stone doorway. I let him. Here, trees hold crumbling temples, vines wrap the faces of holy men set in rock, and the boughs scream with birds. I am bad. When you squabbled, I fed you whiskey until you stooped with drink. When you palpated my breasts, a constant on and off touch, I yanked the hairs on your under belly, pulling them out, follicles and all. When you lead me to your upstairs mat on the floor, I threw your phone, hoping it would shatter. You picked up the phone, said, *Things can't break here,* and something about the empty walls, the floors without support. I said, *Another shot?* Now, he pulls me into the darkness, wound tight by trunks that hold this shrine in place. I am no temple virgin, no cloaked goddess, no troll cursed to live as human. Against the stone, I say cuddle, say kind touch, say tell me good things. He yells in another tongue. He kicks at the roots that hold the door open. Dirt falls. Outside, birds screech in the trees. My sleeve twists in his hands. I can smell his breath. His face chafes my own. I stumble deeper into what's left of the shrine and slide to the floor. I can't breathe. He follows me, turns on a light, illuminating spider webs, words carved in other languages, the blood on my thighs. *I'm here to guide you,* he says, and I think, here the guided are treated like this. Nothing gets inside, nothing gets out—I gasp, throw my head back.

Christopher Howell

    Submitted by Gary Lechliter, who set up the Poets and Poems against Bullies and Bullying Facebook page, where these poems previously appeared, this last one is by Howell. The renowned poet lived in Emporia and knew Phil Miller, a well-known Kansas City poet and poetry promoter for many years.

MEAN AND STUPID

Ricky Stoppard died
in a slimy, undulant tangle
near the south face of a strip mine
outside Weir, Kansas.
That was where the snakes
caught up to him, praying
too loudly and taking the Lord's name
at the same time.
That was how it was.
All the Baptist farmers
hereabouts will tell you
it was a low-down
two-talking son of a loafing skunk
who died that day (riddance be praised!);
that Ricky stank corn liquor,
cursed life, had once attempted armed robbery
of a charity bazaar in Girard, and that the snakes
were instruments of a judgment
others had been making for a long time before the
Almighty
at last threw the machineries of balance
into gear. Rumor
has it too, that Ricky, when he fell
into the fateful waters of reptilian vengeance,
called out for someone to toss him
a brick, thereby adding stupidity to the list of charges.

GIMME YOUR LUNCH MONEY / Christopher Howell

I've seen the gravestone and it reads:

RICKY STOPPARD
1953-1985
Mean & Stupid

I am standing by that tombstone
and my hat is off
to his terrible death
and a life of miserable small crimes
poorly made. I pray I may be spared
the pain and heat of Ricky's soul
that sighed like a rotten wagon wheel
and broke. And I pray for that
soul, the Old Nick of it somehow
near to me as love
or yearning
or any lost equation none of us will ever finally
get. I can hear the night freight
mourning through Riverton
as farmhouse lights die out below the darker
owls circling, flagrantly
disdainful of the Oklahoma line, and Ricky's cruel
headstone comes undone. He's finished now, at least,
and he's all right (being gone). The wind and blown
leaves clatter and agree; at least
he's not all wrong.

—*A New Geography of Poets*
(University of Arkansas Press 1993)

Contributors

Barry R. Barnes (a/k/a Barry Washboard Barnes) is a husband, father, poet, percussionist, performer, zumba instructor, and professional washboard player residing in Lawrence, Kansas. In 2008, Mammoth Publications released his *We Sleep in a Burning House*, a collection of performance poetry.

Roy J. Beckemeyer lives in Wichita, Kansas. His poems have appeared in a variety of regional literary journals including *I-70 Review*, *Kansas City Voices*, *Chiron Review*, *Dappled Things*, *Flint Hills Review*, and *The Midwest Quarterly*, and his first book of poetry, *Music I Once Could Dance To* (Coal City Press 2014) was selected as a 2015 Kansas Notable Book. He won the *Beecher's Magazine* Poetry Contest in 2014, and the *Kansas Voices* Poetry Award in 2016.

James Benger is a father, husband and writer. His work has appeared in several literary magazine, including *Coal City Review*, *I-70 Review*, and *Thorny Locust*. He is the author of the poetry chapbook, *As I Watch You Fade* (EMP 2016). He lives in South Kansas City with his wife and son.

Annette Billings is an award-winning poet from Topeka, Kansas. Her second book of poetry, *A Net Full of Hope*, earned a Topeka ARTSConnect Award for Literature. She also writes short stories and plays. Her chapbook, *Descants for a Daughter*, is forthcoming. Her poetry has been published in Washburn University's *Inscape*, *Kansas Time +Place*, *Liberty Press* and *seveneightfive* magazine. She co-hosts a monthly open mic event, *Speak Easy*, which provides a supportive space for poets to share their work. Known for her dynamic presentation style, she has performed poetry at many venues in Kansas, Missouri, and Nebraska and looks forward to an upcoming event a bit outside the Midwest–in Victoria, British Columbia. For more information, visit her website: http://anetfullofhope.com/Facebook:Facebook.com/anetfullofhope Twitter: Annettebilling3.

A Maine native and former grant manager for the Kansas City Lyric Opera, **Wayne Courtois** lives with his husband, Ralph Seligman, in Kansas City, Missouri. A graduate of the MFA Program at the University of North Carolina-Greensboro, he is author of the memoir *A Report from Winter*, as well as the novels *My Name Is Rand*, *Tales My Body Told Me*, and *In the Time of Solution 9*. His fiction, poetry, and nonfiction have appeared in numerous journals, most recently *Chelsea Station Magazine*, *Assaracus: A Journal of Gay Poetry*, *Jonathan*, and *I-70 Review*. His poetry is also included in the anthology *Hibernation and Other Poems by Gay Bards*.

Pat Daneman lives in Lenexa, Kansas. She has published over 100 poems, most recently in *South 85 Journal*, *Moon City Review*, *Bellevue Poetry Review*, *The Comstock Review*, and on the Escape Into Life art and literature website. In 2015, Finishing Line Press published her chapbook, *Where the World Begins*.

Dennis Etzel, Jr.'s *Fast-Food Sonnets* has just been published (Coal City Press). *The Kansas City Star* named his *My Secret Wars of 1984* (BlazeVOX Books 2015) one of the 10 "Best Reads" for 2015. ELJ Publications released his chapbook, *The Sum of Two Mothers* in 2013. He teaches at Washburn University and holds an MFA from the University of Kansas and an MA and Graduate Certificate in Women and Gender Studies from Kansas State University. His work has appeared in *Denver Quarterly*, *Indiana Review*, *BlazeVOX*, *Fact-Simile*, *1913*, *3 AM*, *Tarpaulin Sky*, *DIAGRAM*, and others. He lives in Topeka, Kansas with his wife, Carrie, who birthed twin boys this spring to join their three other sons.

Gu Jieming Gulley writes, reads, and teaches—among other things. He recently shaved his beard, but it doesn't seem to have affected his writing, not yet anyway. In his free time, he likes to run, ride motorcycles, travel, and watch his cat sleep.

Tina Hacker is a four-time Pushcart Prize nominee whose work has appeared in numerous journals, online and paper. She was a finalist in *New Letters* and George F. Wedge Press competitions and Editor's Choice in two journals. In 2014, Aldrich Press published her full-length collection, *Listening to Night Whistles*, and The Lives You Touch Publications released her chapbook, *Cutting It* in 2010. Tina served as Co-president of The Writers Place in Kansas City, Missouri, and was honored as a "Muse" for that organization in 2016. She also served as Vice-President of the Midwest Region for Women in Communications and received the Matrix Honor prize. Since 1976, Tina has been poetry editor for *Veterans' Voices*, a magazine of writing by veterans nationwide.

A Kansas City Metro native, **Robert Haynes** founded *Lip Service* press, which published a literary journal and sponsored poetry in and around Washington, DC. He also served on the Folgers Poetry Committee and assisted Word Works, Inc., annual Joaquin Miller

Cabin Poetry Series (Summer in the Park). He is author of two poetry collections: *The Next Scene in White Gloves* (Arizona State University 2002) and *The Grand Unified Theory* (Paladin Contemporaries 2001). His poems have been featured on *Verse Daily* and selected as finalists for the Dorsey Prize, Pablo Neruda Prize, and the *New Letters* Award for Writers. Poems have also appeared in *The Bellingham Review, New Letters, Lake Effect, Nimrod, Poetry Northwest, Cimarron Review, Rattle*, as well as anthologies *Cabin Fever, Kansas City Out Loud, Approaching Critical Mass*, and *Important Words*.

Melissa Fite Johnson received her Master's in English literature from Pittsburg State University in Kansas. She was the featured poet in the Fall 2015 issue of *The Journal: Inspiration for the Common Good*. Individual poems have appeared or are forthcoming in such publications as *Valparaiso Poetry Review, Broadsided Press, Rust + Moth, Midwest Quarterly, I-70 Review, Inscape Magazine, 3 Elements Review, Red Paint Hill Journal, Whale Road Review, Bear Review, The New Verse News*, and *velvet-tail*. In 2014, Little Balkans Press released her first book of poetry, *While the Kettle's On*, a Kansas Notable Book and winner of the Nelson Poetry Book Award. Melissa and her husband, Marc, live in Kansas, where she teaches English. Feel free to connect with her at melissafitejohnson.com.

Gary Lechliter's poetry has appeared in *Main Street Rag, New Mexico Poetry Review, Straylight, Tears in the Fence, Wisconsin Review, Begin Again: 150 Kansas Poems, New Letters*, and many other literary journals. Coal City Press has published two of his books, *Under the Fool Moon* (2001) and *Foggy Bottoms* (2007), and in 2014, Woodley Press published his *Off the Beaten Path*.

Denise Low, Kansas Poet Laureate 2007-2009 and AWP board president 2012-13, is author of *Jackalope*, short fiction (Red Mountain Press 2016) and more than 25 books, among them her recent poetry collection, *Mélange Block* (Red Mountain Press 2014). Her memoir, *The Turtle's Beating Heart*, is forthcoming from University of Nebraska Press, 2017. Her website is www.deniselow.net

From Ihie, Abia, Nigeria, **Goldie Manasseh** now lives in Port Harcourt. She studied at the Tago Educational Center and was born on the 31st of July.

Lindsey Martin-Bowen's "Bonsai Tree Gone Awry" in her *Inside Virgil's Garage* (Chatter House Press 2013) was nominated for a Pushcart Prize. The book was a runner-up in the 2015 Nelson Poetry Prize. Her book *CROSSING KANSAS with Jim*

Morrison (in chapbook form) was a semi-finalist in the QuillsEdge Press 2015-2016 Chapbook Contest. McClatchy Newspapers (*The Kansas City Star*) named her *Standing on the Edge of the World* (Woodley Press) one of the *Ten Top Poetry Books of 2008*. Her poems have run in *New Letters*, *I-70 Review*, *Thorny Locust*, *Amethyst Arsenic*, *Flint Hills Review*, *Coal City Review*, *Bare Root Review*, *Rockhurst Review*, ten anthologies, and other literary magazines. She taught at the University of Missouri-Kansas City 18 years and teaches at MCC-Longview.

Ronda Miller enjoys wandering the high plateau of NW Kansas, where the Arikaree Breaks whisper late into the sunsets and scream into blizzards and t-storms. She lives in Lawrence, close to her son and daughter. She was Youth Contest Manager for Kansas Authors Club (2011-2015), serves as District 2 President, Kansas Authors Club and Vice President, the State KAC. Miller is a Life Coach, working with those who lost persons to homicides. Among her widespread poetry credits is her poem in the Smithsonian Institute Archives. Her poetry books include *Going Home: Poems from My Life* and *MoonStain* (Meadowlark Books 2015). In 2010, Miller wrote The 150th Pony Express Reride documentary. She created poetic forms Loku and Ukol, and she dances every chance she gets.

Caryn Mirriam-Goldberg, Ph.D., the 2009-13 Kansas Poet Laureate is the author of 19 books, including *The Divorce Girl*, a novel; *Needle in the Bone*, a non-fiction book on the Holocaust; *The Sky Begins At Your Feet*, a bioregional memoir on cancer and community; and five poetry collections, including the award-winning *Chasing Weather: Tornadoes, Tempests, and Thunderous Skies in Word and Image* with weather chaser/photographer Stephen Locke. Founder of Transformative Language Arts at Goddard College where she teaches, Mirriam-Goldberg also leads writing workshops widely, particularly for people living with serious illness and their caregivers. With singer Kelley Hunt, she co-leads writing and singing retreats. See her work on her webpage at www.CarynMirriamGoldberg.com

Eve Ott's fiction and poetry have appeared in *The Same, Imagination and Place Press*, *I-70 Review*, *The Whirlybird Anthology*, *Kansas City Voices*, *Rockhurst Review*, *Thorny Locust*, *Redbook*, and various campus and regional publications. In 2014, Aldrich Press released her poetry collection, *Album from the Silent Generation*. She is active in the Kansas City literary community as a member of The Riverfront Reading Series Committee, and The Writers Place, and the 365 Poems in 365 Days online Facebook page.

Shawn Pavey is the author of *Talking to Shadows* (Main Street Rag Press 2008) and *Nobody Steals the Towels from a Motel 6* (Spartan Press 2015), Co-founder and former Associate Editor of *The Main Street Rag Literary Journal*, and a former board member and officer of The Writers Place, a Kansas City-based literary non-profit. His poems, essays, and journalism appear in a variety of national and regional publications. A graduate of the University of North Carolina's Undergraduate Honors Creative Writing Program, he likes his Tom Waits loud, his bourbon single barrel, and his basketball Carolina Blue.

Dan Pohl lives in Moundridge, Kansas, and instructs English composition at Hutchinson Community College. Woodley Press published his first book of poetry, illustrated by his daughter Jessie Pohl, *Autochthonous: Found in Place* (2014), which won The Kansas Authors Club Nelson Poetry Book Award in 2014. People can find his work published in two anthologies: *Begin Again: 150 Kansas Poems* (Woodley Press 2011) and *To the Stars through Difficulties* (Mammoth Publications 2012), both edited by past Kansas Poet Laureate Caryn Mirriam-Goldberg. A sampling of his poems is found online at <kansaspoets.com>.

Jeanette Powers is a poet and performance artist based in Kansas City, Missouri. She currently manages the generative performance arts venue, Arts Bar, and also publishes Midwest poets in the Prospero's POP Poetry: #12poetsin12months Series. This year, 39 West Press released her third book of poetry, *Tiny Chasm*. She has been awarded Artist in Residencies at both Osage Arts Community and The Lemon Tree House (Italy) for fall 2016 and she can most often be found on any given nearby river with her kayak and her hound dog, Olly Moss.

Kevin Rabas, Ph.D. chairs the English, Modern Languages, and Journalism Department at Emporia State and leads the poetry track. His seven books include *Bird's Horn*, *Lisa's Flying Electric Piano*, a Kansas Notable Book and Nelson Poetry Book Award winner, *Sonny Kenner's Red Guitar*, also a Nelson Poetry Book winner, *Eliot's Violin*, and *Spider Face: Stories*, and *Songs for My Father*. He writes for Kansas City's *Jazz Ambassador Magazine (JAM)*. His plays have been produced in Kansas, North Carolina, and San Diego. Nominated for the Pushcart Prize five times, his work won the Langston Hughes Award for Poetry, the Victor Contoski Poetry Award, the Jerome Johanning Playwriting Award and the Salina New Voice Award.

Carl Rhoden lives in Lee's Summit, Missouri. He was educated. But no longer. His poems appear sporadically like dust devils.

Ki Russell teaches writing, literature, and creative writing at Blue Mountain Community College in Pendleton, Oregon, where she she resides with her husband Timothy and two children, Rook and Ashe. She serves two cats, Mystique and Nyx and a border collie-blue heeler mix, Dooby, Dooby, Doo. In 2014, Ars Omnia released her experimental novel, *The Wolf at the Door*, a modern fairy tale containing poetry, and Paladin Contemporaries published her poetry collection, *Antler Woman Responds*. Medulla Publishing released her chapbook, *How to Become Baba Yaga* in 2011. She holds a Ph.D. in English literature (creative writing emphasis) from the University of Louisiana at Lafayette and an MA from UMKC.

A retired Special Education teacher, Ecuador-born **Ralph Seligman-Courtois** works as a Spanish/English interpreter and translator. Ralph has translated into Spanish Dr. Don Clark's groundbreaking book *Loving Someone Gay* (*Amar a Alguien Gay*) for Lethe Press. He has also written short stories for several anthologies, including *Tented–Gay Erotic Tales from under the Big Top* and *Tricks of the Trade*. He lives in Kansas City with his husband, author and poet Wayne Courtois and their sweet orange cat, Max.

Tyler Sheldon received his MA from Emporia State University, where he taught English Composition and received the Charles E. Walton Graduate Essay Award. His poems and reviews have appeared in *Coal City Review*, The *Dos Passos Review*, *Flint Hills Review*, *Quiddity*, *Thorny Locust*, and other journals. In May of this year, Oil Hill Press published his debut chapbook, *First Breaths of Arrival*.

Alarie Tennille is a Phi Beta Kappa who graduated from the University of Virginia in the first class allowing women. She is glad to see more public effort directed against bullying. Bullying itself is nothing new, she says. She has encountered it most of her life as sexism. Growing up in the South, she saw racial and homosexual bullying, and her brother was beaten up by bullies in elementary school for being small and smart. It's time to stop, she contends. Tennille serves on the Emeritus Board of The Writers Place. Her first full-length poetry collection, *Running Counterclockwise*, was first runner up in the 2015 Thorpe Menn Award for Literary Excellence. She hopes you'll visit her at alariepoet.com.

Maryfrances Wagner's writings about Italian-American life have been anthologized by Pearson/Longman and others, including *Unsettling America: An Anthology of Contemporary Multicultural Poetry* (Penguin) and *The Dream Book: An Anthology of Writing by Italian American Women* (Syracuse). In 2015, Mammoth Publications released her *Dioramas* and Finishing Line Press published her chapbook, *Poof!* *The Kansas City Star* named her *Light Subtracts Itself* (Mid-America Press) a Notable Book for 2008, and her *Red Silk* (Mid-America Press 1999) won a Thorpe Menn Book Award. Previous poetry collections include *Salvatore's Daughter* (BkMk Press 1995), two more Mid-America Press books, *Tonight Cicadas Sing*, and *Bandaged Watermelons and Other Rusty Ducks* (1978). With Gary Lechliter, Jan Duncan-O'Neill, and Greg Field, she co-edits *I-70 Review*, and her poems have appeared in numerous literary magazines.

Diane Wahto's teaching career spanned from teaching in a one-room country school in Decatur, Michigan, to teaching English, journalism, and creative writing at Butler Community College. Her poems have been published in various journals. Her poem, "Somebody Is Always Watching," won the 1985 American Academy of Poets Award and a first place award in the *American Institute of Discussion Review*. Three of her poems recently won honorable mention in the 2016 Kansas Voices contest. Her 2015 poetry collection, *Leap of Faith*, was designed by her granddaughter Calista Bohling and compiled by her son Curt Bohling. She holds an MFA in creative writing from Wichita State University and lives with her husband, Patrick Roche, and their two dogs, Annie and Mulan, in the Midtown area of Wichita, Kansas.

Laura Madeline Wiseman's recent books are *An Apparently Impossible Adventure* (BlazeVOX Books) and *Leaves of Absence* (Red Dashboard). She is also the author of *Drink* (BlazeVOX Books), winner of the 2016 Independent Publisher Bronze Book Award and *Intimates and Fools* (*Les Femmes Folles*) with artist Sally Brown Deskins, an Honor Book for the 2015 Nebraska Book Award. Her essay on long-distance cycling "Seven Cities of Good" is an honorable mention for the *Pacifica Literary Review*'s 2015 Creative Nonfiction Award. She teaches at the University of Nebraska-Lincoln.

Poetry Books from Paladin Contemporaries

The Dowry of Donna Beach: Songs for a Woman's Voice
by Pat Huyett (1999) (Arvada House Imprint)

Eldorado Rosa: Voices from Midtown
by Pat Huyett (1999) (Arvada House Imprint)

Grand Unified Theory: The Unauthorized Fragments
by Robert E. Haynes (2001)

Antler Woman Responds
by Ki Russell (2014)

CROSSING KANSAS with Jim Morrison
by Lindsey Martin-Bowen (2016)

*GIMME Your Lunch Money:
Heartland Poets Speak out against Bullies*
edited by Dennis Etzel, Jr. and
and Lindsey Martin-Bowen (2016)

"... love one another."
—John 13:34

www.ingramcontent.com/pod-product-compliance
Lightning Source LLC
LaVergne TN
LVHW041631070426
835507LV00008B/556